T0082249

Little People, **BIG DREAMS**™

TERRY FOX

Written by
Maria Isabel Sánchez Vegara

Illustrated by
T. Connor

Frances Lincoln
Children's Books

Little Terry lived in the Canadian city of Port Coquitlam with his parents and three siblings. He was a determined boy who loved all kinds of sports and would never miss a day of school, not even when he was sick.

His favorite game was basketball but, even though he tried his best, he was last to be chosen and played one minute all season. Yet Terry kept practicing and, two years later, he and his friend Doug were valued players on the basketball team.

Being part of a team felt natural to him. So, when his coach encouraged him to try cross-country running, he wasn't sure if he would enjoy running alone. Still, he tried, and soon he was the best distance runner in his school.

He was studying to become a physical education teacher when he noticed a pain in his right knee.

His parent's legs trembled when doctors said it was cancer,
a disease that scientists had long been studying.

Every part of our bodies is made of millions of healthy tiny cells. But some of the cells in Terry's knee were sick, and they were taking up room that belonged to the healthy ones. There was only one way to stop them.

Of course, Terry was very upset about losing his leg. He was worried that he would never walk again. But the night before his surgery, he read the story of a guy called Dick who had run the New York City Marathon with an artificial leg.

That story was like a shining light in the dark! Terry was eager to get up from bed and learn how to use his new leg.

In just three weeks, he was back walking and, a few months later, he and his friend Doug completed a 17-mile-long race.

Terry decided to run across Canada from coast to coast, raising money for cancer research. His goal was to collect one dollar for every Canadian. One spring morning of 1980, under a cold mist, he began running his Marathon of Hope.

Thousands of miles of lonely highways stretched before him, and even though sometimes he felt a terrible pain in his hip, his determination was stronger. Neither the heavy rain nor the sweltering summer heat could stop him!

Soon, the lonely highways were not lonely anymore but filled with people who waited for hours to run next to Terry. Thousands of people cheered for him across Ontario. And, in Toronto, he even met his all-time favorite hockey player.

He had covered more than 3000 miles in five months when he got ill again, and doctors said he needed to go back to the hospital. Terry had to stop running, but he never gave up on his dream. His whole country was there to keep it alive!

People from all walks of life came together to take his place in the battle against cancer. When the first Terry Fox Run was held, sadly Terry was not there anymore, but 300,000 runners joined it and raised millions of dollars for research.

MARATHON OF HOPE CONTINUES

Since then, every September, runners from almost 30 countries all around the world put on their racing shoes and run for little Terry, the bold boy who believed that dreams can be made possible if we all try.

TERRY FOX

(Born 1958 – Died 1981)

1980

1980

Terry Fox was born in Winnipeg, Canada, to a loving family. From a young age, Terry loved sports and he took part in cross-country running and basketball throughout his teens. At only 18 years old, he was diagnosed with osteosarcoma, a type of bone cancer. To try to stop the cancer and save his life, his leg was amputated and Terry was fitted with a prosthetic. Inspired by Dick Traum, the first amputee to complete the New York City Marathon, Terry decided to run a marathon himself. Soon after, he announced to his family that he planned to run the length of Canada to raise money for cancer research. After 18 months of training, Terry was ready to run his "Marathon of Hope." He began in St Johns, Newfoundland, and was greeted by just a few people. But talk of

1980   2014

his feat began to grow, and the Canadian public got behind him.
Running almost 26 miles (42 kilometers) every day, Terry was warmly
welcomed by crowds of people who cheered him on, and he raised
thousands for charity. After 143 days and 3339 miles (5373 kilometers),
Terry was forced to end his marathon early—the cancer had worsened,
making him very sick. Sadly, Terry died at the age of 22 on June 28, 1981.
Even though he didn't finish his marathon, it is estimated that millions of
dollars have been raised in his name. The Terry Fox Run, held annually
in Canada and 30 other countries across the globe, is the world's largest
one-day fundraiser for cancer research. Terry's amazing story shows the
strength of the human spirit, against all the odds.

Want to find out more about **Terry Fox?**

Have a read of these great books:

Terry Fox and Me by Mary Beth Leatherdale

Terry Fox: A Story of Hope by Maxine Trottier

Text © 2022 Maria Isabel Sánchez Vegara. Illustrations © 2022 T. Connor.
Original idea of the series by Maria Isabel Sánchez Vegara, published by Alba Editorial, S.L.U.
"Little People, BIG DREAMS" and "Pequeña & Grande" are trademarks of
Alba Editorial S.L.U. and/or Beautifool Couple S.L.
First Published in the USA in 2022 by Frances Lincoln Children's Books, an imprint of The Quarto Group.
Quarto Boston North Shore, 100 Cummings Center, Suite 265D, Beverly, MA 01915, USA
Tel: +1 978-282-9590, Fax: +1 978-283-2742 **www.Quarto.com**
All rights reserved.

This book is not authorised, licensed, or approved by the estate of Terry Fox.
Any faults are the publisher's who will be happy to rectify for future printings.
A catalogue record for this book is available from the British Library.
ISBN 978-0-7112-7662-8
eBook ISBN 978-0-7112-7661-1
Set in Futura BT.

Published by Peter Marley · Designed by Sasha Moxon
Edited by Lucy Menzies · Production by Nikki Ingram
Editorial Assistance from Rachel Robinson and Lauren Morley-Fletcher
Manufactured in Shanghai, China CC042023
3 5 7 9 8 6 4 2

Photographic acknowledgements (pages 28-29, from left to right): 1. TORONTO, ON: Terry Fox with map in Marathon of Hope van.
Photo taken by Boris Spremo/Toronto Star circa July 30, 1980 © Boris Spremo via Getty Images. 2. Terry Fox, the one legged marathon
runner who won the hearts of Canadians running across the country to raise money for cancer research, smiles after receiving Canada's
highest civilian award the Order of Canada. Terry, who is the youngest ever to be named to the order was presented with the award by
Govenor General Edward Schreyer. © Bettmann via Getty Images. 3. Terry Fox, age 22, is running coast-to-coast across Canada on
an artificial limb, after losing his right leg to cancer three years ago, in an effort to raise money to fight the killer disease. © Bettmann
via Getty Images. 4. Vancouver, Canada. 14th Sep, 2014. Runners take part in The Terry Fox Run 2014 in Stanley Park in Vancouver,
Canada, on Sept. 14, 2014. Thousands of participants pounded the pavement for the 34th time to raise money for the fight against
cancer and to honour the legacy of Terry Fox and his Marathon of Hope. © Sergi Bachlakov/Xinhua via Alamy Images

Collect the Little People, BIG DREAMS™ series:

FRIDA KAHLO	**COCO CHANEL**	**MAYA ANGELOU**	**AMELIA EARHART**	**AGATHA CHRISTIE**	**MARIE CURIE**	**ROSA PARKS**	**AUDREY HEPBURN**

EMMELINE PANKHURST · **ELLA FITZGERALD** · **ADA LOVELACE** · **JANE AUSTEN** · **GEORGIA O'KEEFFE** · **HARRIET TUBMAN** · **ANNE FRANK** · **MOTHER TERESA**

JOSEPHINE BAKER · **L. M. MONTGOMERY** · **JANE GOODALL** · **SIMONE DE BEAUVOIR** · **MUHAMMAD ALI** · **STEPHEN HAWKING** · **MARIA MONTESSORI** · **VIVIENNE WESTWOOD**

MAHATMA GANDHI · **DAVID BOWIE** · **WILMA RUDOLPH** · **DOLLY PARTON** · **BRUCE LEE** · **RUDOLF NUREYEV** · **ZAHA HADID** · **MARY SHELLEY**

MARTIN LUTHER KING JR. · **DAVID ATTENBOROUGH** · **ASTRID LINDGREN** · **EVONNE GOOLAGONG** · **BOB DYLAN** · **ALAN TURING** · **BILLIE JEAN KING** · **GRETA THUNBERG**

JESSE OWENS · **JEAN-MICHEL BASQUIAT** · **ARETHA FRANKLIN** · **CORAZON AQUINO** · **PELÉ** · **ERNEST SHACKLETON** · **STEVE JOBS** · **AYRTON SENNA**

LOUISE BOURGEOIS · **ELTON JOHN** · **JOHN LENNON** · **PRINCE** · **CHARLES DARWIN** · **CAPTAIN TOM MOORE** · **HANS CHRISTIAN ANDERSEN** · **STEVIE WONDER**

MEGAN RAPINOE

MARY ANNING

MALALA YOUSAFZAI

ANDY WARHOL

RUPAUL

MICHELLE OBAMA

MINDY KALING

IRIS APFEL

ROSALIND FRANKLIN

RUTH BADER GINSBURG

MARILYN MONROE

KAMALA HARRIS

ALBERT EINSTEIN

CHARLES DICKENS

YOKO ONO

MICHAEL JORDAN

NELSON MANDELA

PABLO PICASSO

AMANDA GORMAN

GLORIA STEINEM

FLORENCE NIGHTINGALE

HARRY HOUDINI

J.R.R. TOLKIEN

ELVIS PRESLEY

NEIL ARMSTRONG

ALEXANDER VON HUMBOLDT

NIKOLA TESLA

WILMA MANKILLER

MARCUS RASHFORD

LAVERNE COX

MAE JEMISON

DWAYNE JOHNSON

HELEN KELLER

ANNA PAVLOVA

QUEEN ELIZABETH

TERRY FOX

HEDY LAMARR

SHAKIRA

FREDDIE MERCURY

LEWIS HAMILTON

LOUIS PASTEUR

PRINCESS DIANA

DAVID HOCKNEY

VANESSA NAKATE

OLIVE MORRIS

KING CHARLES

Scan the QR code for free activity sheets, teachers' notes and more information about the series at www.littlepeoplebigdreams.com